THE DENOUEMENT

THE DENOUEMENT

A Collection of Poems

BEN WITHERINGTON III

RESOURCE *Publications* • Eugene, Oregon

THE DENOUEMENT
A Collection of Poems

Resource Publications
An Imprint of Wipf and Stock Publishers
199 W. 8th Ave., Suite 3
Eugene, OR 97401

www.wipfandstock.com

PAPERBACK ISBN: 979-8-3852-6312-7
HARDCOVER ISBN: 979-8-3852-6313-4
EBOOK ISBN: 979-8-3852-6314-1

03/30/26

CONTENTS

Contents

PREFACE

Twenty years ago I published an anthology of some of my better poems, but I have continued to write poems since then, so it was time for another collection—-this time mostly poems written since 2006. In that original anthology I said the following which I still feel is apt—-

'Our souls need something positive to contemplate, hopefully something nourishing for the human spirit. The subtitle of this volume "the soul in paraphrase, the heart in pilgrimage" is a line taken from George Herbert's wonderful poem entitled "Prayer (I)." It aptly sums up what is going on in poetry, if it is any good at all. Poetry shows what is on the heart and in the heart, and shows its longings as well—where it is going, or at least would like to go were it able to do so.

'I have been writing poetry since I was a child. It has always seemed a natural means of self-expression to me. This is not a surprise really since I have also been immersed in music all my life, and its lyrical patterns and imprints. Not surprisingly since the music I have been immersed in has been classical music, hymnology, but also popular music of my age (rock and roll and folk music), all of which follow very regular rhythms, my poetry tends to be quite metrical and traditional in character—involving rhythm and rhyme, alliteration and assonance.

'I am not a rap artist or a beat poet. I am a Methodist whose piety is deeply grounded in song, hymn, ode, anthem, oratorio, rock opera, folk ballad and the like. For this reason, those who prefer free verse of various sorts, or avant guard poetry will perhaps need to be patient with what they find here. The test of any good poetry however is not so much its form, but whether the marriage of form and content works, and whether the marriage of self-expression and form is genuine, authentic.

I have accepted long ago that, as these poems show, I am a traditional Christian person who lives a full but orderly life, not usually plagued with huge doubts or the tempests of the soul. My poems reflect the settled convictions by which I live, and they also reflect the fact that I always have some tune or rhythm in my head. I have been told this is one reason I find writing so easy, and it may be so. What I am clearer about is that I write poetry to find out what I am really thinking, feeling, believing, and it is in the articulation that the self-revelation is complete, or at least made clearer.' I hope and trust you will find at least some of the following food for your own hungry souls, and light for your paths.

August 2025

LINDISFARNE LITURGY

(Written in honor of the return of the Lindisfarne Gospels to Durham in the summer of 2013. This poem is written in sprung rhythm following the style of an exemplary English poet—Gerard Manley Hopkins. This poem was written while I was scholar in residence at St. John's College University of Durham)

Was it ever thus, then, and there
So no one need to ask who, when and where
The stones themselves cried out
With the metal bells
That God was in his heaven,
Though some were in their hells . . .

Did it seem quite fixed, fashioned, formed
So few would dare to query, quibble quit
The pilgrimage well trodden
Up the Dun Cow Lane
To Cuthbert's choired cathedral
Saints sang the same refrain . . .

'From holy isle, aisle, I'll
I'll never look away, askance, above
The coffin that souls carried
With the saint within
Told of flesh untainted
By suffering, decay, or sin . . . .'

The monks had come chanting, ranting, granting
Absolution's peace, power, presence.
The river Wear they forded
Afforded a new start
For grace was in the water,
And Spirit in the heart . . .

Illuminated Gospel, Godspell, Godspiel
Good News travelled first, fast, far
As Bede had long intended
Throughout a darkened age
The light would never go out
If shared on Norman stage . . .

And so, the saints keep coming, humming, drumming
The tune that all may hear, fear, revere
Of Yesu who cried Kingdom
And miracles awoke
For God was on his earth
In Christ his master stroke

So let us raise a glass, goblet, chalice
To the Word renewed, returned, reviewed
The lion on the door
Shall give his Dunelm roar
When truth comes marching in
And light is seen once more.

The cathedral in Orvieto, Italy

SOMETHING DEEP INSIDE

Between living and dead
Between heart and head
Between flesh and blood
Between soul and spirit,
Something deep inside.

Between thought and action
Between image and reflection
Between act and being
Between sight and seeing,
Something deep inside.

Between silence and speech
Between grasp and reach
Between alone and lonely
Between singular and only,
Something deep inside.

Between begotten and made
Between art and artifice
Between lost and mislaid
Between offering and sacrifice,
Something deep inside.

Between parent and child
Between Father and Son
Between many and one
Between finished and done,
Something deep inside.

Between union and communion
Between friendship and family
Between sister and brother
Between One and the other,
Something deep inside.

Between loosed and bound
Between circular and round
Between labyrinth and maze
Between fog and haze,
Something deep inside.

Between Spirit and spirit
Between breath and life
Between time and eternity
Between image and identity,
Someone deep inside.

Between appearing and being
Between thought and meaning
Between revery and reverence
Between wholeness and holiness,
  Worship deep inside.

Jan 24th 2005

ANTITHESES

Overweening,
Over bearing,
Just pretending
Never caring
Brash Talk
Trash Talk
Cheap thrills
No frills
Pure bravado
So staccato
Living Large
Not in Charge
LOUD WEAKNESS!

Unassuming
Always daring
Quite authentic
Always caring
Careful talk
Prayerful talk
Real deal
Helping heal
Love in action
Gaining traction
Full of grace
The Master's pace—
Quiet strength.

9-7-07

SILENCE

'Let all mortal flesh keep silence,
And with fear and trembling stand;
Ponder nothing earthly minded
For with blessing in His hand
Peace descends
Our full homage to demand.'

Silence
Is
The Absence of
Sound.

Or
Is it
The presence of
Quiet?

Why
Would silence
Be golden
If it is
Nothing?

Silence
Can only
Be heard
In stillness.

The still
Small voice says
'Be still
And know . . . '

Silence
Has a
Sound
For hearing ears.

Silent prayer
Is
Required
To hear Him.

The heart of worship—
'The Lord is in His House
Let all the earth
Keep silent.'

Silence
Must be *kept*
Like
A precious secret.

Silence
Must be *observed*
If only
For a moment.

Silence
Falls
On a hushed and rapt
Congregation.

Silence
Is
An argument
From
Absence.

Silence
Is a
Pregnant
Pause
So . . . . .

What are you waiting for?

DEPARTURE

Moving, departing, going on ahead
Quitting, exiting, leaving it for dead
Forward motion, progress in a line
Known for the movement, what you've left behind.

Straight as an arrow, now the border bound
Face like a flint set, never looking 'round
Heading for horizon, always gathering speed
Horse and a saddle, all the things you need.

Go west frontiersman, search for better land
Survey, explore, compass in your hand
Scratch the itch, the urge, for going yet again
Never returning, where you once had been.

Facing the sunset, heading now due west
Get there by sundown, or just do your best
Camping out, sleeping rough, now a daily deed
Finding the bluegrass, settling with all speed.

Marksman, surveyor, friend of Indians too
Tar Heel, Kentuckian, knew just what to do
Boon to humanity, and all those he met
A genuine American few have equaled yet

Quaker, hunter, lover of the land
Mason, commander, rifle in his hand
Trapper, trader, family man and then,
Pulled up those stakes, and do it all again.

Born in Penn's woods, died a patriarch
Missouri the last frontier, but Bluegrass in his heart,
Many came after, with succeeding refrain
Ole Dan'el the original, shan't be seen again.

JOB DESCRIPTION

When comfort turns to torment
And solace leads to pain
Then Job will find his master and
Receive his life again.

When ashes without number
Burn on the funeral pyre
Then suffering is consumed
And an end is made through fire.

Yet through the fire a figure
Stands golden, purified
The one who once was taunted
Has now been justified.

Not through the will of mortals
Nor through the countless saints
Can come the vindication
Of Job's quite just complaints.

Let God be God, says Scripture
And all the world be wrong
For triumph comes through suffering
And life from life passed on.

The world has been left hanging
Upon a crooked tree
In Christ the microcosm
Life, through death, is set free.

At Easter dawn a trumpet
Blasts from an empty tomb
Announcing sin's destruction
And death's eternal doom.

" I Know my Redeemer lives
And will stand upon the earth,
And in my flesh I'll see him"
In resurrection's birth.

Darkness lasts a little while
But joy comes with the dawn,
Then Job will see his savior,
And lament will turn to song.

TIME

Time, unmoved but moving
Divider and dividend
Controlling not controlled—
And we often frustrated every minute of it,
Because of these things.

Time,in the final hours of analysis
We may take you—not always by surprise
And give you—the greatest and surest gift—
Time the final currency

To take time to know many things/others
To take time to share many things/ourselves
And so to love each other
Not just the each other in ourselves.

And then to laugh—
When we see the time spent with/on
Others is never costly
When we understand that knowing
Sharing
Loving . . .

Though timed are timeless
And so we too are victors—
Jubilant children set free from father time
Set free by a sense of time
From further restraint—
For the time being— man.

NOVUM ANNUM

Thank Caesar for our calendar
It didn't come from God

It seems so strange we celebrate
The arbitrary, the odd.

Janus at least was two faced
Looking back and ahead.

But we seem to like it better
If we consider the old year dead.

And even the numbered year itself
Comes from a short monk's error.

Jesus' birth did not transpire
After Herod's death and terror.

So what is it we celebrate
With fireworks and with fizz?

Is it the chance to start anew
And redefine what is?

Perchance to be born again,
And this time get it right?

Or a chance to find true love
Turn lonely into light?

Is it a chance to realize
It really could be worse?

You could be homeless or jobless,
Or lying in a hearse.

You could be stuck in prison
With meaningless days to fill.

You could be an abandoned teen
Looking for a thrill.

You could be a drug addict
Who's sold his soul for a hit.

You could be living in a war zone,
Waiting for the end of it.

Where and when you were born
And to whom, you did not choose.

Why should you think that trivial things
Mean that you can't lose.

What if your last name
Is just an accident of birth?

What if your surname
Doesn't reveal your sacred worth?

There are no lucky numbers
Or lucky years at all.

There are no astrological signs
That make you rise or fall.

So much of life is inscrutable
You cannot figure it out.

You have to walk by faith
Even if you're prone to doubt.

If you look at life as a tapestry
That has a divine design,

We look at its back side
Seeking a promising sign.

There seems to be a pattern
But we see it in reverse,

We can't tell which is blessing
And which for sure is curse.

But Christ promised new creation
Because we can't fix ourselves.

He promised a new heaven and earth
The old one's on the shelf.

So perhaps the New Year is a time
To pause and to reflect

We cannot remake our very selves
Or refurbish our old wreck.

Before the final check comes due
Time for a reality check

No use just reshuffling the cards
When it's God who holds the deck.

What we can do is pray
And trust that the One above

Will in the course of coming days
Remake us with his love.

Jan. 1 2015

DIRT

Dirt

Is just matter out of place
It's not innately dirty
It's just in the wrong space.

Soil

Doesn't soil outside in the yard
It's just doing its job
Whether its soft or hard.

Dirt

Is needed just to grow
Even the simplest plant.
And all the food we know.

Soil

Is precious and performs
Necessary functions
Sheltering from the storms.

Earth

It can be dust to dust
But lest we overlook it
It's the genesis of us.

Earthworks

Yes, it surely does.
It is our firm foundation
For all that is and was.

Adam

His name just means earthling
Though disconnected now
Our origin we must surely sing—

Of the ground of all our being
Of the soil in which we grow,
Of the dirt which makes us fertile
Of the earth, the home we know
Of the seedbed of our wisdom
Of the root of all that's strong
Of the raising from the dust,
To the Farmer we belong.

2–25-14

LEAF LEAVING

The veins in the leaf tell a story
Of a glorious chlorophyled past
When the future looked green
As was readily seen
And the leaf thought it would surely last.

But the leaf didn't know it's dependence
On the branch that fed all of those veins
And when the chlorophyl stopped flowing
Color and life stopped going
Leaf leaving, was the Fall's refrain.

The lessons in creation are many
The Creator provides many clues
About our ongoing survival
Life everlasting's arrival
Which to some seems long overdue.

'Abide in me' said the savior
'I'm the way to avoid death's strife'
It requires ongoing remaining
To receive ongoing sustaining
He's the source, the substance, the life.

The sages of old taught from nature
How God's ways could be discerned
'Go to the ant, and scrutinize
Consider its ways and be wise'
Seek sustenance, and you will learn.

In short, learn from the leaf
Or you'll come to grief,
Remain in the vine
And you'll be fine.

9-3-25

PURITY

Purity came down from above
Silently, painfully slow
'Though your sins be red as scarlet
'I'll wash them white as snow'

A gift of unfailing love
That chills one to the bone
Sinking into crevasses deep,
Not leaving unturned one stone.

A pure and penetrating cold
Wind piercing between marrow and spirit
As if the whole person was needing
To experience, to feel, to hear it.

Was needing a complete cleansing
A making of all things new
Not just a surface makeover
But an internal spring-cleaning too.

I stood and watched the cold beauty
And felt it with some alarm
I wrapped my mantle around me
To shield myself from harm.

But a still small voice whispered
In the silence I could barely hear
'Open your heart and your being
And let me wash you clear'

I feared I'd be God's frozen person
I feared an unalterable change
I feared no one would know me
I feared I'd be judged quite strange.

But the snow it just kept falling
An ensign of his constant grace
I unbuttoned my woolen jacket
The flakes fell full on my face.

Purity came down from above
And I gradually let it in
And that has made all the difference,
And yes, I would do it again.

GRAFTON VERMONT

THE PRIORY

The icicles hung on the eaves outside
But the monks were all gone on retreat
The caretaker said 'only God is inside
And there's nothing here you can eat.'

The chapel was silent, oppressively still
The cross hung above the enclosure
Hard benches on the nave's narrow sides
And next to them multiple croziers.

Not a voice in the room, not a bird in the air
The winter wind outside kept blowing
The caretaker said 'Only God is inside'
But if so, why wasn't he showing?

A widow all wizened and totally alone
Entered as if on cat's feet,
Slipping right past me and kneeling right down
She entreated while being discrete.

After time had slipped by, she silently left
A sweet smile creased her old face.
In a voice barely audible, pointing within
'Surely God's inside this place'

——

Sun rose Easter morning casting its pall
The mourners raced to the tomb
The stone was rolled back, no body within
And nothing relieved their gloom.

Yes the tomb it was empty, God wasn't within
But the angels had a strange story
'He's left the building so fear not'
But they fled, struck dumb by glory.

Does presence of absence or absence of presence
Really prove he rose and abides?
Or was it the encounter with Jesus himself
The outsider, who now dwells inside?

——

The bells tolled twice, calling us all to prayer
The sky was stunningly blue
'Inasmuch as he did it for that widow this day,
He'll do it again for you.'

I put on my jacket and braced for the cold,
The caretaker smiled as I passed,
'I told you that God only dwells inside
And I guess you believe me at last.'

At Weston Priory in Vermont

TRUTH SERUM

Is truth like rubber,
Infinitely flexible
Without breaking?

Or is truth like a diamond
Multi-faceted
Refracting pure light
Into many colors?

Or is truth like a brick wall
Unyielding
Something you run into
At your own risk
Realizing you've reached a boundary
That should not be crossed?

Or is truth something ineffable
Something you discover by accident
While in the process of loving someone?
Or is truth unattainable
Something that is clearly out there
And yet you can never full grasp it?

Or is truth irrelevant
To ordinary day to day life
Something only brought up
In rare and necessary circumstances,
When a cure or a conviction is needed?

Is truth bendable
And does it matter when it's bent or manipulated
What changes when that happens?

Or is truth an absolute,
Such that there is no such thing as
My truth or your truth, but only THE TRUTH
Which is universally the same for everyone?

Is truth something that is discovered or recovered
Or believed and received
Does it come like a stone through your mind's plate glass window
Shattering the previous status quo?

But what if truth is a person,
A great I AM.
What if it's not an idea or an abstraction
But a being, in fact THE Being
That founded all things?

What if in the beginning was the Truth
And the Truth was with God
And the Truth was God,
A God to whom all are answerable?

What if no clever questions like
'What is truth'?
Can help a person escape
The claim truth has on them?

What if the alienated
Must make a truce with truth
And the lost must allow themselves to be found
And the jaundiced must be surprised by joy?

What if we are being pursued by truth
All the while we are trying to catch up to it.
And this is so because He is full of grace *and truth?*

And he tells the truth, the whole truth,
And nothing but the truth.
No shadow of turning,
No changing his mind
The same yesterday, today, and forever.

But alas and alack
Can our world ever come back
From being astray
Due to truth decay.

8/1/25

COEUR INCURVATUS IN SE

(as Luther said)

Self-absorbed in the garden
He became Narcissus
The heart inverted
He'll never miss us.

Realized he was naked
Fig leaves won't do,
Hide from your maker,
Who must remake you.

Mirrors and selfies
Self-focus supreme
Who cares about others
If I'm my own dream

The three persons I love
Me, myself, I
I'm always distant
From others who try

To win my attention
To woo me again
To shatter the mirror
To destroy primal sin

The problem with falling
In love with your self
It's a monotonous courtship
A life on a shelf.

It leaves you alone
And lonely as well
It's not self-fulfilling
It's the pathway to hell.

No one is an island
A wise man once said
It's a decline into darkness
It leads to the dead

Yet we long for relations
For love that is true,
But this requires an other
What's a narcissist to do?

Somewhere long ago
A sage made so clear
'You must be born again'
The kingdom is near.

The old self must die,
To have life everlasting
It requires more than just trying
More than just fasting.

You need an intervention
An unlikely hero
A demolition man
And I don't mean Nero.

A radical rescue
Is what is required
A total surrender
Of what self desired.

Not a self-help program
Not five easy steps
Not multiple meditations
Not endless good reps.

Take up *your* cross
Not mine, Jesus said
Would you rather be living
Or carry on dead?

Not self-fulfillment
Self-sacrifice
Is what's required
Is the full price.

The cure for heart disease
In our deadly condition
Is a total transplant
By the great physician!

January 4, 2025

BOXING DAY

[**Boxing Day** is a holiday celebrated after Christmas day, occurring on the second day of Christmas tide (26 December). *It originated as a holiday to give gifts to poor people.*

On Boxing Day
We give it away,
The things we do not want,

We wrap it up
And raise a cup
To those who can't or don't

But what if
Instead we gave
The thing we value most?

What if we gave
A costly gift
Needed from coast to coast?

What if a sacrifice
Is what
This day requires?

Not leftovers
Or duplicates
Or things we don't admire?

What if tangible things
Are good
but not good enough?

What if love and joy
Is more
Than material stuff?

On Boxing day
We need to say
I'm here without conditions

On Boxing day
We need to display
Love—much more than traditions.

It is in giving
That we receive
It is in living
What we believe—

That Christ is the gift that keeps on giving
On this and every day,
You keep his love within your life
By joyfully giving it away.

BW3 12/20/23

BLOOD VESSELS

Chalice, Cup
Grail, Goblet
Waiting Wine Glass—
Blood Vessels.

Plate, Patin
Wafer, Morsel
Beckoning Bread basket—
Table service.

Mere morsels
Or bare Body?
Uncommon Cup
Or Challenging Chalice?

From Sacrifice
To Sacra meant
From Sign to Symbol
From Serving to Service
Grace Comes a Calling

Blood Shed
Blood Transfusion
His Extinction
Our Restinction
By Intinction? 'You Are What You Eat (or Drink?)'

IMITATIO CHRISTI

(in memoriam—Thomas A Kempis May 1, 1471)

The cruciform life to which we are called
In the crucible of life we give you our all
Shaped and sharpened
Enlightened and lead
In the footsteps of Him
Who rose from the dead.

By dying to sin and living anew
We boldly embody Immanuel who—
Through his grace has brought us,
With his word has taught us,
By his blood has bought us,
        — Lord Jesus Christ.

May 1, 1990

'DEATH BE NOT PROUD'

Death came unexpectedly,
And uninvited too
It left us lost, wondering
What's a soul to do.

You realize you're helpless
And have no final say
You've lost control quite quickly
And it's too late to pray

Yet death can be a mercy
Instead of endless pain
Life's not endless sunshine
But it shouldn't be just rain

I miss my friend quite deeply
It chills me to the bone
One moment we're together
And now I'm quite alone.

Where's the world where death has died
And we don't live in fear
Because we are quite mortal
The shadow creeps too near

But death is not final
Can't have the final say
It has its pyrrhic victory
That lasts but for a day

The prophets promised lasting life
That buries even graves
And carries on eternally
Because the Maker saves

And not just new humans
But new creation too
All creatures great and small
Can all be made anew

Meanwhile I am in mourning
Not like those who have no hope
The night can't last forever
I'll climb that final slope

And see with joy renewal
Redemption, rescue too
Wolves and lambs together
And humans made brand new

A world resurrected
Sin, sorrow, suffering gone
Disease, decay are banished
Creation carries on

The river of life flows through it
The trees with leaves that heal
And what seemed a dream to many
Has become the realest real

So I'll not say goodbye now
To my departed friend
Instead I'll say 'au revoir'
And look beyond this end.

For Minnie
2/6/24

FINALLY

The presence of her absence
Was noted by them all
They waited to hear her familiar walk
Or her southern drawl . . .

The silence wasn't deafening
In fact, it spoke a lot,
It meant they were remembering
What they had forgot

In deference they waited
And hoped to hear a sound
But not even a whisper
Came from the burial mound

Death can seem quite final
With someone whom you love
Your heart keeps on yearning
Even when she's gone above

The birds were singing cheerfully
It seemed so out of place
The world should be mourning
Not just the human race.

The flowers kept on blooming
The sun refused to hide
The cars just kept on moving
And took it all in stride

But the family was quite silent
Standing in the cold
Hoping for renewal
But feeling oh so old.

But then the words came telling
A very different tale
That life's final victory
Will one day prevail

Ashes to ashes
And dust to dust, they say
In sure and certain hope
Of resurrection's day

4/9/23— Easter. BW3

HARMONIES HARMING ME

Is it consonant or dissonant
Do memories fade away
Or are they silently edited
So memories are here to stay?

And yet, I cannot erase
The horror of seeing her face
In a coffin . . . .
My Christy girl gone
Now for far too long.

The night of her death
Took away my breath,
A dark cloud descended
No use if I pretended.

While such wounds
May gradually heal,
They leave a permanent scar
Tender, to touch and feel.

Unbidden grief returns
Through hearing a familiar song
That Christy loved singing,
But the echo is gone before long.

An unexpected blending
Of sorrow and joy unending
Consolation can be condescending
Is resurrection death's rescinding?

Someday I'll know as I am known
Someday I'll see face to face
Besides the vision glorious
I hope reunion takes place.

PARENTHOOD

Parenthood's a mirror
Revealing all your flaws
You try to repress them
A rebel with a cause

But it does not work, it cannot work
Because despite it all
Those flaws just keep appearing
Like writing on a wall.

So, you divert attention
To things you do quite well
To avoid listening to the voice
That has that truth to tell

You revel in successes
That don't involve your child
You ignore their plaintive calling
'Spend time with me awhile'

You rationalize and realize
You thought it was God's call
To do all these other things
As most important of all.

You hear a Harry Chapin song
About a traveling Dad
Who avoided his child's play
And made his son quite sad.

What goes around, comes around
And now the child's a man
With a father asking for his time
And the son says- 'someday I can'

Perhaps you should have listened
When the poignant poet cried:
'The saddest words of tongue or pen
What might have been, what might have been'

BW3. 3/31/23

LENTEN LEXICON

It's not the blood lines
Or the age lines
That define the man

It's the thought lines
And the taught lines
That refine the man

It's not the clothes
Or the shows
That finally make the man

It's the devotion
And emotion
That reveal just who I am

I'm not a product once assembled
Or a willow in some gale
I'm the writer who listens
To the Author of our tale

——

It's not the consumer
Or consumption
For you're not what you eat

It's Who caught you
And bought you
That's made you complete

It's not a moving target
Or a flash before one's eyes
For life's more than we realize.

It depends on an embrace
Of truth amongst the lies
Or else a tragic mess.
Unfolds before our eyes.

I'm not a victory
Or defeat in someone else's story
I'm the teller of His tale
That finally ends in glory

We become what we admire
Or so the wise man said
Who gave his life for us
Then rose up from the dead.

BW3. Jan. 24, 2023

RSVP

To move from fast to feast,
From ashes to riding an ass,
From wilderness wandering
God's willingness wondering
To follow the way of the cross
To find what was utterly lost
All this was Lent to us.

The cup not passed over
By our Passover
The vinegar he willingly drank—
But through gift divine
New covenant wine
Came forth from his side as he sank
All this was given to us

Through breaking of bread
They knew their head
The joy of new life begun
From out of the depths,
From out of his death
His people one loaf had become
All this was food for us.

Lent leads to Easter
The faster turns feaster
A foretaste for those in the dust
A bread with new leaven
The manna from heaven
        All this has risen for us.

God's ways are not our ways,
Our eyes cannot see,
The logic of love,
Nailed to a tree.
Come now to the dinner
Come saint and come sinner,
        The meal is now served to us.

Lent 1982

THE ALCOVE

A niche,
A hideaway
A retreat
A sanctuary

For prayer
Communion
Contact
Reunion

Like the horns on the altar
Like the hem of his robe
Like the songs in the psalter
Like his hand on the globe

Like a vault for safekeeping
Like a treasury found
Like a library of answers
Like a truth that's profound

One God
One sinner
One entreaty
One answer

Forgiveness
For peace
For wisdom
Release

A secret space
A closet
A meeting place
An alcove.

"But when you pray, go into your closet, close the door and pray to your Father, who is unseen. Then your Father, who sees what is done in secret, will reward you. Do not keep babbling on like pagans, for they think they will be heard because of their many words. Do not be like them, for your Father knows what you need before you ask Him. This then is how you should pray . . . 'Our Father . . . .' Dec. 2005

This magnificent painting of the moment when the woman with the blood flow is healed is in the basement chapel of the new Franciscan church at Migdal, and was painted by Daniel Cariola. I've been fortunate enough to be there several times and take pictures, and reflect on that amazing miracle. That chapel surely is such an Alcove.

TRIVIAL PURSUIT?

Trivial,
Tiny,
Miniscule,
Small.

'Unimportant',
Ignored,
Neglected
By all.

Overlooked
Out of sight
Out of mind
Yet real

Atoms,
Molecules
Quarks
A big deal.

Why would
We assume
Small's
Insignificant?

Why would
We assume
Tall's
Magnificent?

Humans
Miniscule
Compared
To the earth.

But this is
Hardly
A measure
Of worth.

Small
Holds
Together,
Much of the rest.

Details
Matter
History
Suggests:

"For want of a nail,
The horse was lost,
For want of the horse,
The message was lost

For want of the message
The battle was lost,
For want of the battle,
The war was lost,
And all for the want of a nail."

Minutiae
Matters
As it all
Turns out.

Attention
To detail
Helps things
Work out.

Study
The small things
Get down
To the root.

God's
In the details
Hardly
Trivial pursuit.

Dec. 7 2005

CRACKS IN THE WALL

Cracks in the wall,
There by design,
Prayers on plain paper
One of them mine
Rabbis are chanting,
Torah held high,
Sunlight is fading,
In the blue sky.
Guards are watching,
Passing the time,
Nodding acquaintance
With the sublime.

Herod's temple,
All that remains
Limestone platform,
Withstands the strain,
Mosque's gold dome
Shines in the light,
Whose God is honored
By what's in sight?
Prayers of the righteous
Meant to be heard,
But the papers are silent,
Say not a word.

“We want messiah”
Yeshiva boy cries,
The irony is thick,
And darkens the skies

Christians with kepas
Stand by the shrine,
Praying to Jesus,
As someone divine.

The wailing wall,
Heard Jesus’ lament
That he would have gathered,
If Zion would repent.

Cracks in the wall,
Filled up with our prayers,
Perhaps it is this,
Which keeps God right there
Perhaps when Messiah
Comes (once again),

Perhaps then the Spirit
Will descend through the air,
Perhaps then true monotheists
Will kneel at God’s feet,
Be filled with his Spirit,
The Father’s Son greet.

True children of Abram
Meet at the wall
And confess Trinity,
The One for us all.
Is this a dream— we three could be one?
Just as God is,
Whose plan is not done.
"Something there is
That doesn't like a wall"
But this one unites
The One with us all.

9/11/05

LIFE LONG/ LONG LIFE

(for family and friends)

Sadness sinks in,
With the passing of the past
Great ones

Their voices are not silenced
Since they are on record and records

But there is no fresh work
No new thing to bring the Spring
Of the heart
The elation of creation
The thrill of live and embodied
The erection of connection

Between artist and audience
Between musician and the music
Between time and eternity.

Sometimes the sounds resound
Fill the soul and move the self,
But sometimes we say . . .
Can these bare bones live
What do they have to give

But a pale shadow
A fleeting glimpse
An awakened memory
That dwells on the past
And cannot last?

Can we face the past
Backing our way into an uncertain future?
Backing our way
Down the corridor of today?
Can we face the music
That we are all timed beings
And say honestly . . .

'Out out brief candle,
Life is but a poor player
That struts and frets its time upon the stage
And is no more'

Or should we *carpe diem*,
Not merely *carpe the per diem*
Or is there something greater than merely lasting
Or outlasting others,
Could there really be everlasting?
Not just everlasting creations
But everlasting creatures?

My heart says yes
My mind says yes please
My soul says there must be
More in store for the timed being

So, for the time being
I remember these words—
'Ashes to ashes
Dust to dust,
In sure and certain hope of the resurrection'

I reach out my hand in faith—
Faith the assurance of things hoped for,
And a strong conviction about the things
Not yet *seen*
But I can almost *hear* the heavenly choir
That my heart desires

And think here how to tune my instrument
So that I will be in tune when I get there . . .
Beyond the river, beyond the earth, beyond the air,
In a permanent somewhere,

Where there is no suffering, sin, or sorrow
No disease, decay or death
Where never is heard a discouraging word

No more crying, no more tears
No more hatred, no more fears
No more weakness, no more worry
No more haste, no more hurry

But faith becomes sight, hope is realized
And love endures forever
In the presence of the One who is Love.

So instead of saying farewell
To parents and friends who have gone before
I say Fare Well,
And when I cease to roam,
I'll see you at Home.

6/12/23

MYSTERIUM

They say it is a 'mystery'
A puzzle in a phrase
But is it revelation
Which always will amaze?

They find the 'mystery' lacking
Clear diction and quite plain
And if it causes pondering
They're going to complain.

Where is the love of eloquence
In form and substance too
Must discourse be plebian
In order to get through?

Not all things in the Bible
Are clear to one and all
And when the truth's apparent
Sometimes it will appall.

Clarity is a virtue
But sometimes it offends
The sense and sensibility
Of enemies and friends

Who wants an intruding truth
That upsets a quiet life
And changes one's direction
The result—unending strife.

The preacher's great temptation
In trying to please the crowd
Is over-simplifying
And repeating it too loud.

But life is complicated,
And there's mystery in Good News
It serves no good purpose
To trivialize the truths.

There is a need for reflection
Some truths are hard to grasp
The learning curve is steep
The light may dawn at last.

Perhaps perspicuity
Is not lacking in the Word
But in the puzzler's brain
To whom it seems absurd.

Beware the proclaimer
Who thinks he knows it all
And can unveil the mystery
Of Redemption and the Fall.

We see through opaque windows
And comprehend in part
It requires ongoing repentance
And an open heart.

And when it becomes apparent
Our flaws have been revealed
The kind of illumination
Unsought but oh so real.

Like a two-edged sword
Piercing our facade
In learning God's message
We learn we're far from God.

So ponder God's witness
And learn about your state
We fall short of God's glory
My destiny or my fate?

Or perhaps a unique providence
Governs our lives and call
And we are saved by grace
Not by knowing all.

The *mysterium tremendum*
Once heard and seen and felt
Should humble us for certain
Forgiveness is what we're dealt.
Sola deo gloria
BW3 —8/28/24

CONNUNDRUM

I've lost faith in my faithfulness
But I need to be needy,
I would like to be liked
And I wish I had less wishes

I've given some thought to my thoughtlessness
I'm not patient with my impatience
I say I love the loveless,
But it's the loveable that gets my attention.

Am I just a bundle
Of endless contradictions
Or is my assessment
Right about my convictions?

When does intellectual rigor
Become just an exercise
Am I over analyzing
Navel gazing, in disguise?

Is rigor *rigor mortis*
A refusal to ever change
Or is apparent honesty
Evidence you are strange?

Perhaps Elgar's *Enigma Variations*
Will provide me with a clue,
Of how to settle unsettledness,
And know just what to do.

Don't listen to the con man
Who makes conundrums seem true
The power of self-deception
Should be evident to you.

THE HARBINGER

Quite quiet
Unexpectedly
The Harbinger appears
Foreshadowing or foretelling
Events of coming years.

But for good or ill?
The image is opaque
The Harbinger relates
Some kind of news
But first or second rate?

Hindsight seems much clearer
The Harbinger does not
A most unwelcome warning
The future's unclear
Like shadows before morning?

But if its undetermined
Then there's time to make a change
Time to make amends
For wrongs that have been done,
Repent for all our sins.

The Harbinger's a sign
Of what one day *may be.*
It's not all pre-planned
Awaiting our clear response
By every woman, every man.

Hovering on the horizon
Like sunrise every day
The Harbinger demands attention
A responsible response
Intervention and prevention.

Reading the signs of the times
Is no easy task,
It requires a steady gaze
While looking for the sun
To daze or to amaze?

Most prognosticators
Are usually mostly wrong
They sing a sad lament
Will the future bring disaster
Or is it heaven sent?

The Harbinger is like a whisper
You barely hear and fear
Is something creeping up on us
Despite our best intentions
Should we ignore the fuss?

Who was it sent the Harbinger
Perhaps some evil spirit
Who seeks to do us harm?
Or was it God Almighty
Not a false alarm?

This much I know for certain
Beyond my reasonable doubt
Not knowing *how* the future goes
I know *who* holds it in his hands
And that's all I need to know.

BW3
12/13/24

THE HARBINGERS OF FALL

The harbingers of Fall
Are warnings to us all,
It's downhill from here
Despite how it appears.

There's no point complaining
About the dying of the light
No point maintaining
That things are just as bright.

Instead, there's beauty in the falling
As leaves complete their calling
To live and then to die
Like sunsets in the sky

There's no point in regretting
What's gone forever more
But remember, not forgetting
What yet we have in store.

For seasons have their reasons
Don't call it nature's treason
For in dying they're reborn
On a crisp Springtime morn.

Perhaps they are reminders
That we have cycles too
And though we face our dying
Our story is not through.

BW3
8/4/23

SHADE TREE

A tree always a tree,
That shadows forth his shade to me.

The tree of Eden long before
Tempting those who longed for more
Knowledge, power, experience,
But lacking trust, lacking sense.

A tree, always a tree
That shadows forth his shade to me.

The burning bush
Could Moses see
More than curiosity
Ablaze with all infinity.

A tree always a tree
That shadows forth his shade to me.

That terrible Terebinth
Oh Absalom, a tithing tenth
Ensnared in branches as he went,
The royal robe of David rent.

A tree, always a tree,
That shadows forth his shade to me.

Elijah lost and on the run
A broom tree shading from the sun
He prayed to die but fell asleep
And angel's food his soul did keep.

A tree always a tree
That shadows forth his shade to me.

Ezekiel's cedar of Lebanon
Which once was here but now is gone
Cut down by ruthless foreign foes
A symbol of the chosen's woes.

A tree always a tree
That shadows forth his shade to me.

Moaning Jonah could not see
In a tree-like vine, God's mercy
And so it withered and it died,
And Jonah sulked and Yahweh cried.

A tree always a tree
That shadows forth his shade to me.

Isaiah saw Eden's door
Fertile fig trees, no more war

But exiles failed to take the hint
Returned to fight, hope misspent.

A tree always a tree
That shadows forth his shade to me.

The cursed fig of Jesus' day
Sign of judgment on the way
Blighted when it bore no fruit
Unplanted souls without a root

A tree always a tree
That shadows forth its shade to me.

The cross a tree on which he hung
Bore the curse of which they sung
'His ways are not ours, our eyes can not see,
The logic of love nailed to a tree.'

A tree always a tree
That shadows forth his shade to me.

And then at last Jerusalem
Where rivers flow and kingdoms come
The tree of life, twelve fruits it bears
Medicinal leaves that heal the cares.

A tree always a tree
That shadows forth his shade to me.

CREATURES OF HABIT

Creatures of habit,
Day after day
Go about life,
The same old way.

Nothing disturbs
Their orderly routine
All must be neat,
And all must be clean.

They're making their lists
And checking them twice,
Trying to make sure
Their work will suffice.

Impatient by nature
They don't suffer fools
Gladly or otherwise
Because of the rules.

A place for everything
For all there's a place
Don't touch the guest towels
But please wash your face.

They insist on living
Orderly lives,
And of course only marry
Orderly wives.

Their homes antiseptic
Their cars always clean,
Their food always healthy
Their meat always lean.

Like ants in an ant hill,
Repeating their tasks
Rest in repetition
Ignore the mask.

Chaos is forbidden
Experiment absurd
Don't ask for creative
Don't mention the word.

Creatures of habit,
By whose design?
Is this just human,
Or is it divine?

What if we found
That ordering our sphere,
Is just a misnomer
For controlling our fear?

Fear of the truth,
Fear of falling
Fear of the unknown,
Fear of our calling

Fearing to let go,
Fearing to try,
Fearing to live,
And fearing to die.

Perhaps if we surrender
Control of our lives,
And offer ourselves
To all seeing eyes

We'd find a new freedom
Though not out of bounds
For when he controls us
The order's profound.

Let go of the death grip,
You have on your life
Inhibit your habits
Without artifice.

Accept serendipity,
Free by design
Eat the new manna
Drink the new wine.

Come to the manger
Kneel at the throne
Realize your ruler
Won't leave you alone.

Celebrate Christmas
Deliverance declare
You're freed to inhabit
A creature's full share.

Dec. 1 2005

THE BONDING

A cold and listless season,
And full of cheerless cheer,
When hopes are raised and dashed again
And joy dissolves in tears.

The search for endless family
The search for one true Friend
Leaves questers tired, disconsolate
With questions without end.

Best find some potent pleasure quick
Some superficial thrill
Than search for everlasting love
When none can fill that bill.

So hide yourselves in shopping
And eating 'til you burst,
Use endless entertainment
As shelter from the worst.

And hope at least for truce on earth,
Though warlords rattle swords
As if to kill could solve our ills
We seize our 'just' rewards.

Mistake some rest for lasting peace
And calm for 'all is well'
And absence of activity
As year end's victory bell.

But what if Advent is no quest
Despite the wise men's star
What if Advent isn't reached
By driving from afar?

What if Good News comes to us
From well beyond our reach?
What if love and peace on earth
Are more than things we preach?

What if a restless peace
Is what He did intend
Until we open up our lives
And let the stranger in?

What if a peaceless rest
Is not the Christmas hope
What if nothing we could do
Helps us truly cope?

What if there is a bonding
With one who rules above
Who came to us in beggar's rags
And brought the gift of love?

The God shaped hole in every heart
Is healed by just one source
When Jesus comes to claim his own
Who are without recourse.

So give up endless seeking
Surrender is required
The one who is the Lord of all
Cannot be bought or hired,

He's not conjured into life
By pomp and circumstance
By Yuletide carols boldly sung
By fun or drunken trance.

He comes unbidden, unawares
Fills crevices of souls
He comes on his own timely terms
And makes the sinner whole.

'We shall be restless' said the saint
'Until we rest in thee'
And find that we have been reborn,
Our own nativity.

How silently, how silently
The precious truth is given
And God imparts to human hearts
The blessings of his heaven.

OPUS MAGNUM

Weary, worn, welts on hand
Work has whittled down the man
To the bare necessities
Of what he is, and what he'll be
Was this then his destiny?

Defined, refined by what we do,
The toilsome tasks are never through
Thorn and thistle, dirt and dust
Sweeping clean, removing rust
All to earn his upper crust?

Sweat of brow, and carried weight
Rose too early, slept too late
Slaving, striving dawn to dusk
Til the shell is barely husk
Staunch the stench with smell of musk?

But work is not the curse or cure
By which we're healed, or will endure
It will not save us in the end,
It is no foe, but rather friend
But while it molds us will we mend?

Task Master making all things new
Who makes the most of what we do,
Let our work an offering be
A timely gift from those set free
From earning our eternity.

When work is mission on the move
By those whose efforts serve to prove
That nothing's wasted in God's hands
When we respond to his commands
Then we shall hear him say "well done"
To those who worked under the Son.

Oct. 4, 2005

A KNOTTY PROBLEM

The knot in my stomach
Wouldn't go away
Because she was gone,
Because she could not stay.

One day we were celebrating
My 60th birthday
A few days later
She was found
on her stone-cold floor
Stone cold.

Her dogs lay beside her
Waiting to go out
Waiting for her to arise
But she had already gone out . . .
Without them
Without us.

Death is a mystery
We cannot understand
Even as a transition
For every woman and man

Did life stop
Or where did it go
Must we follow
Or can we say no?

Why does it seem so final
A coda that has to end
Or is it just our viewpoint
That will not let us in

Into the wonder
Into the gate
Into the Presence
Before it's too late

Perhaps just a glimpse of glory
Perhaps a foretaste
Would be enough to sustain us
Without any waste

But then I remembered
What the Master had said
She is just sleeping
Not really dead,

I cannot wait
For her Easter day
When I hear him say
Death passed away.

For Christy . . . .Twelve years on.
Feb. 2. 2024

'IS JUSTICE JUST ICE'[1]

They say that might makes right
Those who bear the sword,
Not so says the king of kings
Who rules by just his Word

What might happen to the world
If power was used for mercy
And riches to feed the poor,
If living and dying by the sword
Was banished forever more?

Might should serve the right
So righteousness prevails
All the power in the world
Misspent, cannot avail.

Kingdom rise and kingdoms fall
Due to the pride of men
And ego rears its ugly head
And shouts 'I have no sin' . . .

And wickedness wins again

Ben Witherington

1. This is all the more a question today, now that we have people in masks called ICE snatching people they assume are illegal immigrants, without due legal process. One estimate says less than 10% of those detained have committed any crimes.

CHANGED

"Changed.
I say I'm changed.
Ironing out one's deepest wrinkles
Isn't strange."

"Gone.
Perhaps gone on.
Those wanderlusting feelings
Once so strong."

"Clear.
Horizon's clear.
I see where I must go
While standing here."

"Hope.
That helps me cope.
Even though I've started down
The dark and dusty slope."

"Resolved.
To not look back.
In longing or in anger
And get off track."

"Possessed.
Not a possessor.
By a Spirit not my own
I'm made confessor."

"Consumed.
Not a consumer.
There's room for growth
In a late bloomer."

"Changed.
But for the better.
The Giver has tranformed
A greedy getter."

In short——
Spotless leopards can adapt
Old dog saying isn't apt.

For my Father on his 90th birthday— May 31 2006

GLORIOUS ANACHRONISMS?

To look back in anger is pointless,
For the past cannot be changed

To look back in longing is fruitless
For you cannot resume or rearrange

Your memories are selective
The looking glass view doesn't last.

—

While we cannot live in the past
We shouldn't even try

If we attempt to do so
The world will pass us by

Glorious anachronisms are curiosities
But they only deserve a glance

Amish buggies get our attention
But then we look askance.

—

Meanwhile all around us keeps changing
Adapt or fall victim to chance.

There is nothing so permanent as change
With one outstanding exception

The Lord is the same forever
Look to him for your future direction.

—

Artificial intelligence won't save the human race
No one can take our real Savior's place.

www.ingramcontent.com/pod-product-compliance
Lightning Source LLC
LaVergne TN
LVHW050540100826
845148LV00002B/629